The Social Evolution of the Black South

By

W. E. BURGHARDT DU BOIS

Copyright © 2023 by BLP PUBLISHING

BLP PUBLISHING
Eastchester New York

For wholesale please visit:
www.BBWLogistics.com

Available wherever books are sold.

ISBN: 978-1-63652-174-9

# THE SOCIAL EVOLUTION OF THE BLACK SOUTH

Edited By
W. E. BURGHARDT DU BOIS

# CONTENTS

W. E. Burghardt Du Bois

# DR. W. E. BURGHARDT DUBOIS.

Dr. W. E. BURGHARDT DUBOIS is a native of Great Barrington, Mass. After receiving an education in the schools of his native city he entered Fisk University, Tennessee, from which he graduated with the degree of A. B. He subsequently graduated from Harvard and received the degree of Ph. D. He obtained a scholarship and studied two years abroad. Returning to the U. S., he entered upon a distinguished career both as an educator and author. He taught at Wilberforce University, and for more than ten years was Professor of History and Political Economy in Atlanta University. Dr. DuBois is editor of the "Crisis," the organ of the National Association for the Advancement of the Colored People.

W. E. Burghardt Du Bois

# The Social Evolution Of The Black South

W. E. Burghardt Du Bois

# THE SOCIAL EVOLUTION OF THE BLACK SOUTH

I HAVE worded the subject which I am going to treat briefly in this paper; "The Social Evolution of the Black South," and I mean by that, the way in which the more intimate matters of contact of Negroes with themselves and with their neighbors have changed in the evolution of the last half century from slavery to larger freedom. It will be necessary first in order to understand this evolution to remind you of certain well known conditions in the South during slavery. The unit of the social system of the South was the plantation, and the plantation was peculiar from the fact that it tended to be a monarchy and not an aristocracy.

In the early evolution of England we find men of noble and aristocratic birth continually rising and disputing with the monarch as to his arbitrary power and finally gaining, in the case of Magna Carta, so great influence as practically to bind the monarch to their will. In France on the other hand we find continually a tendency for monarchs like Louis XIV to gain such power that they forced even the aristocracy to be their sycophants, and men who, like the rest of the monarch's subjects had no rights which the monarch was bound to respect.

We must now remember that the little plantations which formed the unit of the social life in the South before the war tended continually to the French model of Louis XIV and went in many cases far beyond it, so that the ruler of the plantation was practically absolute in his power even to the matter of life and death, being seldom interfered with by the state. While, on the other hand, the mass of field hands were on a dead level of equality with each other and in their surbordination to the owner's power. This does not mean that the slaves were consequently unhappy or tyranized over in all cases, it means simply what I have said, they were at practically the absolute mercy of the owner. The real owner could be a beneficent monarch—and was in some cases in the South—or he might be the brutal, unbridled tyrant—and was in some cases in the South. Just where the average lay between these two extremes is very difficult to determine with any degree of accuracy but the experience of the world leads us to believe that abuse of so great power was in a very large number of cases inevitable.

Turning now to this great army of field hands we find them usually removed one or two degrees from the ear of the monarch by the power of the overseer and his assistants. Here again was a broad gate way for base and petty tyranny. The social life on the plantation, *that is*, the contact of slave with slave was necessarily limited. There was the annual frolic culminating in "the Christmas"; and there was usually a by-weekly or monthly church service. The frolic tended gradually to demoralization for an irregular period, longer or shorter, of dissipation and excess. Historically it was the American representative of the dance and celebration among African tribes with however, the old customary safeguards and traditions of leadership almost entirely gone, only the dance and liquor usually remained. The church meeting on the plantation was, in its historical beginning, the same. Just as the Greek dance in the theatre was a species of a religious observance in its origin and indeed in its culmination so the African dance differentiated: Its fun and excesses went into the more or less hidden night frolics; while its tradition and ceremony was represented in the church services and veneered with more or less Christian elements. Of the distinctly family social life, the whole tendency of the plantation was to leave less and less.

Polygamy was established and to some extent encouraged into the West Indies and its opposite was not systematically frowned upon in America, and there was neither time nor place for family ceremonial. There was a common sleeping place more or less confined to a family; a common eating place but few family celebrations. Sometimes there was a ceremony of marriage but this was an exception among the field hands. There was certainly no ceremony of divorce and little authority over children. The whole tendency of the plantation was toward communism of eating, children and property.—Facts which show their definite results among us to-day—some good and some bad. The beautiful hospitality, for instance, among our poorest Negroes and the willing adoption of orphan children is balanced against bad systems of eating and living and illegitimate births. In and over all these plantation organizations there must of course have arisen that thing so characteristic of monarchal power, namely, the tale bearer and the thief. The man who curries favor by telling on the neighbors, and the man who having no chance to earn what he wants, steals it. From tale-bearing and deception on the one hand and unusual ability and adaptability on the others there arose from the dead level of the plantation field hands two classes of incipient aristocracy, namely, the artisan and the house-servant. The artisan by natural and acquired manual and mental dexterity coupled with more or less keenness of mind became a slave of special value. On his ability the whole plantation to a large extent depended. He built the houses, he repaired them, made and repaired most of the tools, arranged the crops for market; manufactured the rolling stock. As the plantations increased and were systematized he became so valuable that he was an article of special barter and could by shrewdness himself dictate often the terms of his use. Many stringent laws were mimed against him to keep him from becoming too independent. Nevertheless he increased in numbers and sometimes bought his own freedom. In many cases he acquired property. He was demanded in large and larger numbers in the cities and he formed a growing problem of the slave system. He is the direct ancestor of the city Negro. Side by side with the slave mechanic and in some cases identical with him arose the house-servants; as the mechanic gained his power by ability and economic demand the house-servant gained a more tremendous and dangerous power by personal contact until on some plantations it was actually a question as to whether the master would rule his servants or his servants rule him, but when such a statement is made it must be interpreted as applying to the house-servant and the house-servants were but a small per cent of the total number of slaves; because the house-servant gained very intimate knowledge and opportunity to serve the good will and even the affection of the master or to pander to his vices and because too from the house-servants the great amalgamation of the races took place so that the servant was often blood relative of the master. In this way the house-servant became even a more dangerous person than the mechanic.—More dangerous because he could command a more careful protection of his master a more intimate protection, and because he inevitably had chances for education which the mechanic did not. When therefore, emancipation came it found the cultured house-servant further on the road to civilization, followed by the less cultured but more effectual artisan and both dragged down by the great unnumbered weight of largely untouched field hands. The great change which freedom brought to the plantation was the right of emigration from one plantation to another but this right was conceded by no means everywhere and is not even until this very day. Gradually, however large and larger numbers of field hands changed plantations or migrated to town. In the change of plantations they slowly but surely improved the rate of compensation and conditions of work, on the other hand, they remained and still remain so far as they stayed on the plantations, a backward uneducated class of servants except where they have been able to buy land. And even there they have become efficient, pushing and rising only in cases where they have education of some degree. Now it was the Negro that migrated to town that got a chance for education, both in early days and largely so to-day. In town he met the school and the results of the school, i. e., he himself learned to read and write and he came in more or less contact with the things and influence of men who had learned more than mere reading and writing. We must then if we would know the social condition of the Negro to-day turn our attention to this city group. No matter how much we may believe the country the place for the Southern Negro or stress its certain advantages to him there, the sad truths remains that the black man who can take advantage of these opportunities is represented in the country districts in very small numbers and cannot under present circumstances be represented by larger numbers save through conscientious, systematic group effort. It is the city group of Negroes, therefore that is the most civilized and advancing and it is that group whose social structure we need to study. It is in the south above all a segregated group, and this means that it is the group that lives to itself, works by itself worships alone and finds education and amusement among its own. This segregation is growing, and its growth involves two things true in all evolution processes, namely, greater differentiation and greater integration. Greater differentiation from the white group in, for instance, the schools of the city which it inhabits, the interests which attract it; the ideals which inspire it and the traditions which it inherits. On the other hand greater integration in the sense of stronger self consciousness, more harmonious working together with a broader field for such co-operation. We often compare the North and South with regard to these things and pointing to the tremendous co-operation of the southern city group we urge the Northern group to follow its foot-steps without stopping to think that tremendous and even harsh differentiation must precede and accompany all such integration and in so far as that differentiation is absent in the North, it is this absence here that it gives a chance for a slower but larger integration in the North which may in the long run, and already has, helped the smaller intenser integration of the black Southern group. Now to illustrate just what I mean by the integral life of the Southern group let me point the possibilities of a black man in a city like Atlanta to-day. He may arise in the morning in a house which a black man built and which he himself owns; it has been painted and papered by black men; the furniture was probably bought at a white store, but not necessarily, and if it was; it was brought to the house by a colored draman; the soap with which he washes might have been bought from a colored drug store; his provisions are bought at a Negro grocery; for the most part his morning paper is delivered by a colored boy; he starts to work walking to the car with a colored neighbor and sitting in a part of the car surrounded by colored people; in most cases he works for white men, but not in all, he may work for a colored man or a colored family; even if he works for a white man his fellow workmen with whom he comes in contact are all colored; with them he eats his dinner and returns home at night; once a week he reads a colored paper; he is insured in a colored insurance company; he patronizes a colored school with colored teachers, and a colored church with a colored preacher; he gets

�│uented and usually run by colored
ﾉ a colored undertaker in a colored
⸍tion of the city few or no white people live,
children grow up with colored companions; in
ᵥhite person seldom if ever enters; all the family
⸍nusements and ceremonies are among his own people.
⸍ such a situation means more than mere separation from
ᵥhite people; it means, as I have intimated before, not simply
separation but organized provision for the service of this colored
group. The group must see to it that religion, education, amuse-
ments, etc., are furnished its members, and while some of these
things are left to chance more and more such groups are consci-
entiously exerting themselves to provide for themselves in these
ways and this is what I mean by integration. The place, however,
where the separation cannot be made perfect is in matters of
work in economic co-operation and here the Negro in this city
group occupies one of two very different positions: he may be
and often is one of those who is engaged in service which the
group as such demands, i. e., a teacher, a lawyer, a physician, a
druggist, an artisan whose clients are colored or a servant for
colored people. This group of employees are growing rapidly
but it is a small group and a group naturally paid relatively small
wages. On the other hand, the great mass of this city group are
persons whose employment makes them a part of the whole

economic organization of the South and Nation. These
great mass of laborers, porters, servants and artisans.
contact with the white group is considerable and constant a
that contact enters and necessitates continual existence of so
intercourse. It is here that the great battle of the race question
being fought. But fought as you will perceive, not by the most
highly educated and able members of the group but, usually, by
the middle class workingman and very often too the tendency is
rather to separate that group of men from its natural intellectual
leaders; This in the Southern city group of yesterday was
possible, but is to-day being made more and more impossible
because these natural leaders are seeking economic improvement
as leaders of the integrating forces of the race. They depend,
therefore, for their enumeration upon this mass of workingmen
and upon the loyalty with which this mass of workingmen co-op-
erate in organization. They must, therefore, cater to the whims
and likes and dislikes of the mass of the Negro people. This
makes physicians and their kind, like teachers, preachers and
lawyers drawn to the mass of their people by strong cords of
self-interest because their bread and butter lies in the masses
hands, while on the other hand, this same mass is tremendously
dependent upon this intellectual aristocracy for such organization of their life as will make their life pleasant and endurable.
Consequently there has grown up in the new South among the

city groups certain well defined social classes with comparatively few social chasms. Roughly speaking, there is a large middle class of working people; an upper class of professional people and a lower class of the poor and semi-criminal. The upper class find their social intercourse among themselves and in contact with the mass of laborers whom they meet in church, in the lodge, in the school and neighborhood and in the streets. The middle class of laborers have most of their social contact with themselves, occasional contact with their own upper class and also a large semi-social contact with the whites through their occupations as house-servants, artisans, porters, etc. The last class of the very poor and semi-criminal have little or no contact with their own people outside their own class but a very large and a very intimate contact with certain classes of whites. Now these facts are perfectly real to one who knows the South and are true in some degree of Northern cities, but they lead to certain results to which few people give intelligent thought. Namely: in case the white group wishes to communicate with the Negro group its only method of communication is through the middle class of workingmen. The white people of Atlanta *do not know* the colored teachers, physicians, lawyers or merchants. They *do* know the servants, the porters and the artisans. They are therefore, continually led to assume that the Negroes whom they do not know or meet are either nonexistent or are quite a negligible quantity. They do not realize *first* that there is a group of greater education and ability than they have met right in their own midst and *secondly* they do not realize that that higher group is an organ unit with the mass of workingmen, and that consequently it is quite impossible to deal to-day with the mass of Negroes without taking this upper class into account. Then again the poor and semi-criminal class looms large in the eyes of the white community because of their dependence and their delinquencies, and when there comes the question of the reformation or proper punishment of this class the white community is at an utter loss as to where to appeal. They see with perfect justice that the Negro laborer although himself honest is not capable of bearing the burden of reforming his criminals. The whites themselves cannot do it because they lack the human contact and charity. They consequently make no trial and leave this class to be abused by the economic and social exploitation of their own worst white elements. This but inflames and degrades and makes worst the Negro criminal classes. On the other hand, the upper class of Negroes has no way of communicating with its white neighbors at any rate of speaking with sufficient authority, so that these whites will realize that they are at least the nucleus of the class who can deal with the problem of race contact and crime. This then in brief is the situation. What now is the mental attitude engendered by it?

The chief results among both blacks and whites is evidence of peculiar moral strain. A strain which does not always voice itself; indeed which finds it difficult to choose words, but a strain nevertheless which is manifested in a hundred different ways. Both white men and black men try to hide it. Ask a black man about conditions in the South and he is evasive; he speaks upon this and that pleasant point but of the whole situations of the general trend he does not wish to speak, or if he does speak his speech is difficult to understand. Precisely the same thing in differing ways is true of the white man, and it leaves the outside spectator peculiarly puzzled. The fact is that both black and white in the South endure the present pain and bitterness but see a wonderful vision. The black man endures segregation and personal humiliation but sees the development and unfolding of a human group, one of the most fascinating and inspiring of spectacles. The white man endures the moral contradiction of conscious injustice and meanness, but sees the vision of a white world without race problems where all men can really be brothers with an intense yearning for democracy but democracy upon certain terms. With them the evil and the vision, there must be among both black and white a daily and hourly *compromise*. The black man can daily balance things and say "Is the vision of a strongly developed race worth the present insult, or blow or discrimination?" The white man must say "Is the promise of a real democracy worth the present lie and deception and cruelty?" The necessity of these daily compromises leads to three sorts of mental attitudes among both races. The man who sees the situation clearly and lies about it; the man who sees the situation and resents it; and the man who does not clearly understand the circumstances and is silent and sensitive under the ruthless conditions.

Among the first of these three attitudes is the wily and oily orator who attends Northern chautauquas and tells of his love for his black mammy; the brutal hot-headed brawler and lyncher who wants to fight a desperate cause but takes it out in fighting the helpless; and finally the man who typifies what is called the "silent South". On the part of the Negro there are avowed also the three types: the wiley and crafty man who tells the North and the Negro of the kindness of the South and advance of the black man; the fighter who complains or shoots or migrates; and the silent sensitive black man who suffers but says nothing. Now of these three types I am free to say that the one of whom I hope most is the white brawler and the black fighter; I mean by that not that lynching is not horrible and fighting terrible but I do mean that these are types of men of a certain rough honesty.

Your Tillmans and your Vardamans represent a certain disgusting but honest ignorance which acts upon its information and some day when it gets the right information it is going to act right. On the other hand, I believe that at the end of the devious way of the compromiser and liar lies moral death.

I do not believe that the systematic deception concerning the situation in the South either on the part of white men or black men will in the long-run help that situation a single particle. I sincerely hope, therefore, that out of the white silent South and from the ranks of the silent and sensitive Negroes will come men who will approach the lyncher and fighter with their barbaric honesty of purpose and will bring to the situation that large knowledge and moral courage which will enable them to say that *this is wrong* in the South and *that is right*, and *I am fighting for the right*; who will stoop, if necessary, but will let no man ever doubt but that they stoop to conquer.

*9 7 8 1 6 3 6 5 2 1 7 4 9 *